Dedication

To all those who ever struggled with learning a foreign language and to Wolfgang Karfunkel

Copyright © 2015
Yatir Nitzany
All rights reserved
ISBN-13: 978-1951244057
Printed in the United States of America

CONVERSATIONAL RUSSIAN QUICK AND EASY SERIES

The Most Innovative Technique to Learn the Russian Language

YATIR NITZANY

Foreword

For many years I struggled to learn Spanish, and I still knew no more than about twenty words. Consequently, I was extremely frustrated. One day I stumbled upon this method as I was playing around with word combinations. Suddenly, I came to the realization that every language has a certain core group of words that are most commonly used and, simply by learning them, one could gain the ability to engage in quick and easy conversational Spanish.

I discovered which words those were, and I narrowed them down to three hundred and fifty that, once memorized, one could connect and create one's own sentences. The variations were and are *infinite*! By using this incredibly simple technique, I could converse at a proficient level and speak Spanish. Within a week, I astonished my Spanish-speaking friends with my newfound ability. The next semester I registered at my university for a Spanish language course, and I applied the same principles I had learned in that class (grammar, additional vocabulary, future and past tense, etc.) to those three hundred and fifty words I already had memorized, and immediately I felt as if I had grown wings and learned how to fly.

At the end of the semester, we took a class trip to San José, Costa Rica. I was like a fish in water, while the rest of my classmates were floundering and still struggling to converse. Throughout the following months, I again applied the same principle to other languages—French, Portuguese, Italian, and Arabic, all of which I now speak proficiently, thanks to this very simple technique.

This method is by far the fastest way to master quick and easy conversational language skills. There is no other technique that compares to my concept. It is effective, it worked for me, and it will work for you. Just be consistent with my program. By learning these mere 350 words, which I will teach you in this book, you too will also succeed the way I and many, many others have.

Contents

Introduction to the Russian Language............................ 6

Russian Pronunciation... 7

The Program... 8

Building Bridges.. 41

Useful Vocabulary 48

Note from the Author... 52

Also by Yatir Nitzany.. 53

The Russian Language

As many Russian words have Bulgarian roots, Russian is the most common language in Europe and Russia. Perhaps a reason for its popularity is that it also derives vocabulary and connotations from the French, English, German, Latin, and Greek languages. It is also one of the official languages of United Nations. After the Soviet Union fell apart, Russian was only the official language of present-day Russia, and other countries that were part of the Union were encouraged to speak their native tongues. Prior to that, all countries that were part of the Soviet Union were required to speak only Russian, though it still remains the official language of Ukraine, Kazakhstan, Kyrgyzstan, and Belarus. However, Russian is not limited to Europe, as it is the tenth most-spoken language in the United States.

Spoken in: Russia, former Soviet republics

RUSSIAN PRONUNCIATION

In this program, whenever encountering a *t'* at the end of verbs, pronounce it as a soft "ts." For example, "to buy" / *kupit'* is pronounced as "kupits" (with a soft sounding "ts").

Whenever encountering *y'y* or *u'u*, pronounce them as "uo" as in "buoy."

Kh—For the Russian language as well as Middle Eastern languages, including Arabic, Hebrew, Farsi, Pashto, Urdu, Hindi, etc., to properly pronounce the *kh* or *ch* is essential, for example, *nacht* ("night" in German) or *Chanukah* (a Jewish holiday) or *Khaled* (a Muslim name). The best way to describe *kh* or *ch* is to say "ka" or "ha" while at the same time putting your tongue at the back of your throat and blowing air. It's pronounced similarly to the sound that you make while clearing your throat of phlegm. *Please remember this whenever you come across any word containing a *kh* in this program.

Again, this is *not* a pronunciation book. The sole purpose of this book is to provide you with the necessary skills in order to engage in fluent conversational communications. With regards to grammar and pronunciation, you are *on your own!*

The Program - *Let's Begin! "Vocabulary" (Memorize the Vocabulary).*

I / I am - Ya Я
With you – S toboy С тобой
With us - S nami С нами
For you - Dlya tebya Для тебя
For you - (**Plural**) dla vas для вас
You - (**informal**)Ty Ты
You - (**formal**)vy вы
You - (**plural**)vy вы
Are you / you are - (**informal**)Ty Ты
Are you / you are - (**formal**)vy вы
Are you / you are - (**plural**)vy вы
From - (from a place) Iz Из
From - (from person) ot от
Today - Sehodnya Сегодня
House / home - Dom Дом
Russia - Rossiya Россия
Moscow - Moskva Москва

Sentences composed from the vocabulary you just learned.

Are you at the house?
Ty doma?
Ты дома?
I am always with her
Ya v'segda s ney
Я всегда с ней
I am from Russia
Ya iz Rossii
Я из России
Are you from Moscow?
Ty iz Moskvi?
Ты из Москвы?

Disclaimer: This program doesn't address the nominative, accusative, genitive, dative, instrumental, and prepositional cases since, as it was previously stated, this isn't a grammar book.

With him - S nim С ним
With her - S ney с ней
Without him - Bez nego Без него
Without them - Bez nih Без них
Always - V'segda Всегда
The - (no equivalent)
This, this is - (Masc) Etot Этот
This, this is - (Fem) Eta Эта,
This, this is - (Neuter) Eto Это
This, this is - (Plural) Eti Эти
These – Eti Эти
Better - Luchshe Лучше
He, he is - On Он
She, she is – Ona Она
Sometimes – Inogda Иногда
Alone - Odin один
Was - Byl Был
No - Net Нет
Yes - Da Да

Are you alone today?
Ty odin segodnya?
Ты один сегодня?
This is for you
Eto dlya tebya
Это для тебя
Sometimes I go with him
Inogda ya idy s nim
Иногда я иду с ним
I am with you
Ya s toboy/ ya s vami (plural)
Я с тобой/ я с вами

*In Russian, the article "the" doesn't exist nor do the verbs "is" and "are." The article "a" doesn't exist in Russian either.

I was - Ya byl Я был
To be - Byt' Быть
Good/ Okay - Khorosho Хорошо
Here - Zdes' Здесь
Here - Vot вот
Very - Ochen' Очень
And - i (pronounced as ee) и
Between - Mezhdu Между
If - Yesli Если
Now - Sey'chas Сейчас
Same - Tozhe samoye Тоже самое
Tomorrow - Zavtra Завтра

I was here with them
Ya byl zdes' s nimi
Я был здесь с ними
I was home at 5pm
YA byl doma v 5 vechera
Я был дома в 5 вечера
Between now and tomorrow.
Mezhdu seychas i zavtra.
Между сейчас и завтра.

*In regards to the adjectives "this," "that," "its," and "these," if there is a word between these adjectives and the noun, then use eto это. However, if these adjectives are followed by a noun, then their conjugation is according to gender and/or singular and plural: etot этот(m.), eta эта(f.) eto это(n.), eti эти(p.).
"this/that is a girl" / eto devushka это девушка, "this/that girl" / eta devushka эта девушка, "these are girls" / eto devushki это девушки "these girls" eti devushki эти девушки, "this/that is a boy" / eto mal'chik это мальчик, "this/that boy" etot mal'chik этот мальчик, "these are boys" / eto mal'chiki это мальчики "these boys" eti mal'chiki эти мальчики.

The Program

Day - Den' День
It's - **(M)**Etot Этот
It's - **(F)**Eta Эта
It's - **(N)**Eto Это
It's - **(P)**Eti Эти
Later / After - Pozzhe Позже
Later / After - Posle после
Later / After - Pozdno поздно
Yes - Da Да
Then - Zat'em Затем
Good - (person) **(M)**Khoroshiy Хороший
Good - (person) **(F)**khoroshaya хорошая
Happy - Schastlivyy Счастливый

You and I
Ty i ya
Ты и я
It's better to be home later.
Luchshe byt' doma pozzhe.
Лучше быть дома позже.
If this is good, then I am happy.
Yesli eto khorosho, to ya schastliv.
Если это хорошо, то я счастлив.
Yes, you are very good
Da, ty ochen' kharoshiy/kharoshaya
Да, ты очень хороший/хорошая
The same day
Tot zhe den'
Тот же день

*In Russian, whenever "what" is preceded by a noun, you say kakoy какой. <u>kakoy</u> какой(m.) / <u>kakaya</u> какая(f.) / <u>kakoe</u> какое(n.) / <u>kakie</u> какие(p.)

Maybe - Mozhet byt' Может быть
Even if - Dazhe yesli Даже если
Afterwards - Posle После
Afterwards - Potom потом
Worse - Khuzhe Хуже
Where - Gde Где
Everything - (**person**) vse все,
Everything - (**object**) vsyo всё
Somewhere - Gde-to Где-то
What - Chto? Что?
Almost - Pochti Почти
There - Tam Там

Even if I go now
Dazhe yesli ya idu seychas
Даже если я иду сейчас
Where is everything?
Gdé vs'o?
Где всё?
Maybe somewhere
Mozhet byt' gde-to
Может быть где-то
Where are you?
Gde ty?
Где ты?
What is this?
Chto eto?
Что это?
This is for us.
Eto dlya nas.
Это для нас.
Where is the airport
Gde aeroport
Где аэропорт

The Program

Good morning - Dobroye utro Доброе утро
How are you? - Kak dela? Как дела?
Where are you from? - Otkuda ty Откуда ты?
Hello / hi - Zdravstvuyte Здравствуйте
Hello / hi - Privet привет
What is your name? - Kak tvoyo imya? Как твое имя?
How old are you? - Skol'ko tebé lét Сколько тебе лет?
House / home - Dom Дом
In / at – V В / na на

Good morning, how are you today?
Dobroye utro, kak samochuvstviye?
Доброе утро, как самочувствие?
Hello, what is your name?
Privet, kak tebya zovut?
Привет, как тебя зовут?
How old are you?
Skol'ko tebe let?
Сколько тебе лет?
Where are you from?
Otkuda ty?
Откуда ты?
Is this place near?
Eto mesto ryadom?
Это место рядом?
I want to sleep
Ya khochu spat'
Я хочу спать
Where is the book?
Gde kniga?
Где книга?

*In Russian, na на mean "at," "in," "at the." However, v в could have a similar meaning, but it mostly refers to "inside": "at (inside) the mall," "in (inside) the car."

Car - Avtomobil' Автомобиль
Car - Mashina машина
Already - Uzhe Уже
Me - Mne Мне
Son – Syn Сын
Daughter - Doch' Дочь
Daughter - Dochka дочка
Your - Vash Ваш
Your - Tvoy твой
But / however - No Но
Hard - (hard object) Zhostkiy Жосткий
Hard - (difficult) Trudnyy трудный
Still - Yeshcho Ещё
Before – Pered Перед
Before – do togo до того
Yesterday - Vchera Вчера
For - Za За
For - (a person) Dlya Для

She is not in the car, so maybe she is still at the house?
Yeyo net v mashine, tak chto, mozhet byt', ona vse yeshche doma?
Её нет в машине, так что, может быть, она все еще дома?
I am already in the car with your son and daughter
Ya uzhe v avtomobilye s vashim synom i dochkoy
Я уже в автомобиле с вашим сыном и дочкой
This is very hard, but it's not impossible
Eto ochen' trudno, no eto ne nevozmozhno
Это очень трудно, но это не невозможно
He was here yesterday.
On byl zdes' vchera.
Он был здесь вчера.

*In Russian, "what is your name?" is kak tvoyo imya? как твоё имя? Informally, this is kak tibya zovut? как тебя зовут? while formally it is kak vas zavut? как вас зовут?

The Program

Thank you - Spasibo Спасибо
That, that is - (M)Etot Этот
That, that is - (F)Eta Эта
That, that is - (N)Eto Это
That, that is - (P)Eti Эти
Time - Vremya Время
Not - Ne Не
I am not - Ya ne Я не
Away - Daleko Далеко
Late - Pozdno Позно
Similar - Analogichnyy Аналогичный
Similar - Pokhozhiy Похожий
Our - Nash Наш
Other / Another - (M)Drugoy Другой
Other / Another - (F)drugaya другая
Side - Storona Сторона
Until - Do До
Without us - Bez nas Без нас

Thank you, Anton.
Spasibo, Anton.
Спасибо, Антон.
I am not here, I am far away
YA ne zdes', ya daleko
Я не здесь, я далеко
That house is similar to ours.
Etot dom pokhozh na nash.
Этот дом похож на наш.
I am from the other side
Ya s drugoy storony
Я с другой стороны
I was here last night
Ya byl zdes vchera vecherom
Я был здесь вчера вечером

I say / I am saying - Ya govoryu Я говорю
What time is it? - Skol'ko vremeni? Сколько времени?
What time is it? - Kotoriy chas? Который час?
I want - Ya khochu Я хочу
Without you - Bez tebya Без тебя
Everywhere - Vezde Везде
I go / I am going - Ya idu Я иду
With - S С
My - (**M**) Moy Мой
My - (**F**) moya моя
Light – Svet Свет
I need - Mne nujno Мне нужно
I see / I am seeing - Ya vizhu Я вижу
Right now - Seychas Сейчас
To - Dlya Для

I am saying no / I say no
Ya govoryu net
Я говорю нет
You need to be at home.
Tebe nuzhno byt' doma.
Тебе нужно быть дома.
I see light outside
Ya vizhu svet snaruzhi
Я вижу свет снаружи
What time is it right now?
Skol'ko vremja seychas?
Сколько время сейчас?
I see this everywhere
Ya vizhu eto vezde
Я вижу это везде

*This isn't a phrase book! The purpose of this book is solely to provide you with the tools to create your own sentences!

The Program

Night - Noch' Ночь
Evening - Vecher вечер
Cousin - (**M**)Dvoyurodnyy brat Двоюродный брат
Cousin - (**F**)dvoyurodnaya sistra двоюродная сестра
To see - Videt' Видеть
Outside - Snaruzhi Снаружи
I must - Ya doljen Я должен
During - Vo vremya Во время
Happy - (**M**) Schastliv Счастлив,
Happy - (**F**) Schastliva Счастлива

I am happy without any of my cousins here
YA schastliv bez moikh dvoyurodnykh brat'yev zdes'
Я счастлив без моих двоюродных братьев здесь
I want to see this in the day
Ya khochu uvidet' eto dnyom
Я хочу увидеть это днём

*In Russian, pronouns have different conjugations when relating to gender:
- "her": yeyo её, his: yego его, its: yego его / he: on он, she: ona она, it: ono оно, they: oni они
- "my": moy мой (male), moya моя (female), moyo моё (neutral), moi мои (plural)
- "their": ikh их (same for male, female, formal, informal, and neutral)
- "your": tvoy твой (male), tvoya твоя (female), tvoyo твоё (neutral), tvoi твои (plural) / "your" (singular formal or plural): vash ваш (male), vasha ваша (fem), vashe ваше (neuter), vashi ваши (plural)
- "our": nash наш (male), nashi наша (female), nashi наше (neutral), nashi наши (plural). Note: *Moikh Моих* is the genitive as well as plural accusative form of the pronoun "my." This program doesn't address the nominative, accusative, genitive, dative, instrumental, and prepositional cases since, as it was previously stated, this isn't a grammar book.

Place - Mesto Место
Easy - Legko Легко

To find - Nayti Найти
To look for /to search - Iskat' Искать
Near - Okolo Около
Close - Ryadom Рядом
To wait - Zhdat' Ждать
To sell - Prodat' Продать
To use - Ispol'zovat' Использовать
To know - Znat' Знать
To decide - Reshit' Решить
Between – Mezhdu Между
That - (conjunction) Chto Что

This place is easy to find
Eto mesto lehko nayti
Это место легко найти
I want to wait until tomorrow
Ya khochu podozhdat' do zavtra
Я хочу подождать до завтра
It's easy to sell this table
Etot stol lehko prodat'
Этот стол легко продать
I want to use this
Ya khochu ispol'zovat' eto
Я хочу использовать это
Is it possible to look for this book in the library.
Mozhno li poiskat' etu knigu v biblioteke.
Можно ли поискать эту книгу в библиотеке.
I need to know that everything is ok
Mne nuzhno znat' chto vsyo v poryadke
Мне нужно знать что всё в порядке

*In the last sentence, "that" is used as a conjunction, chto что.

The Program

Because - Potomu chto Потому что
Them - Ikh Их
They - Oni Они
Their - Ikh их
Mine - Moyo Моё
To understand - Ponyat' Понять
Problem - Problema Проблема
Problems - Problemy проблемы
I do / I am doing - Ya delayu Я делаю
To do - Sdelat' Сделать
Like this - Tak так
I can - Ya mogu Я могу
To work - Rabotat' Работать

Do it like this!
Delay eto tak!
Делай это так!
That book is mine
Eta kniga moya
Эта книга моя
I need to understand the problem
Mne nuzhno ponyat' problemu
Мне нужно понять проблему
I can work today
Ya mogu rabotat' segodnya
Я могу работать сегодня
I am there with him
Ya tam s nim
Я там с ним

*In Russian, the verb "need" can either be nuzhno нужно or dolzhen должен, occasionally they can be used interchangeably. However, nuzhno нужно is mostly used to signify necessity while dolzhen должен is used to signify being forced to do something.

To buy - Kupit' Купить

Both – Oba Оба
Each / Every – Kazhdyy Каждый
Myself - Sam Сам
Food - Yeda Еда
Water - Voda Вода
Hotel - Otel' Отель
I like - Mne nravitsya Мне нравится
Your - Tvoy Твой
To look - Smotret' Смотреть
To look - Iskat' искать
Outside - Snaruzhi Снаружи
Of – Iz Из

I like this hotel because it's near the beach
Mne nravitsya etot otel', potomu chto on ryadom s plyazhem
Мне нравится этот отель, потому что он рядом с пляжем
I want to look at the view.
YA khochu posmotret' na vid.
Я хочу посмотреть на вид.
I want to buy a bottle of water
Ya khochu kupit' butylku vody
Я хочу купить бутылку воды
I have a view of the city from the hotel
Iz' moyego otelya vid na gorod
Из моего отеля вид на город
I can go outside.
YA mogu vyyti na ulitsu.
Я могу выйти на улицу.

*In Russian, posmotret' посмотреть is "to look" (all around) while smortet' смотреть is more focused.

*In Russian, the definition of nravitsya нравится is "to enjoy."

The Program

Parents - Roditeli Родители
Why - Pochemu Почему
To say - Skazat' Сказать
Something - Chto-to Что-то
Ready - Gotovo Готово
Soon - Skoro Скоро
To work - Rabotat' Работать
Who - Kto Кто
There is / There are - Yest' Есть

I like to be at home with my parents
Mne nravitsya byt' doma s moimi roditelyami
Мне нравится быть дома с моими родителями
Why do I need to say something important?
Zachem mne govorit' chto-to vazhnoye?
Зачем мне говорить что-то важное?
I am busy, but I need to be ready soon
Ya zanyat, no ya dolzhen byt' gotov skoro
Я занят, но я должен быть готов скоро
I like to work
Mne nravitsya rabotat'
Мне нравится работать
Who is there?
Kto tam?
Кто там?
I want to know if they are here.
YA khochu znat', zdes' li oni.
Я хочу знать, здесь ли они.
There are seven dolls
Yest' sem' kukol
Есть семь кукол

*In Russian, moimi моими is the instrumental form of the pronoun "my."

How much - Skol'ko stoit Сколько стоит
To take - Vzyat' Взять
With me - So mnoy Со мной
Without me - Bez menya Без меня
Instead - Vmesto Вместо
Only - Tol'ko Только
When - Kogda Когда
I can - Ya mogu Я могу
Can I - Mogu li ya? Могу ли я?
Or - Ili Или
Were - Gde Где
To eat - S'yest' Съесть
To drink - Vypit' Выпить
I love Ya lyublyu Я люблю

How much money do I need to bring with me?
Skol'ko deneg mne nuzhno vzyat' s soboy?
Сколько денег мне нужно взять с собой?
I like to eat bread instead of rice.
YA lyublyu yest' khleb vmesto risa.
Я люблю есть хлеб вместо риса.
Only when you can
Tol'ko kogda ty mozhesh'
Только когда ты можешь
Go there without me.
Idi tuda bez menya.
Иди туда без меня.

*In Russian, whenever pluralizing nouns, the ending changes to an i. For example, "book" / kniga книга, when pluralized, becomes knigi книги. In Russian, in regards to the verb "need" / nuzhno нужно, its ending changes to an i as well whenever indicating plural possession: "I need the books" / mne nuzhny knigi мне нужны книги or "he needs the books" / Emu nuzhny knigi Ему нужны книги, etc.

The Program

To Drive - Vodit' Водить
Fast - Bystro Быстро
Slow - Medlenno Медленно
Cold - Kholodno Холодно
Hot - Goryacho Горячо
Inside - Vnutri Внутри
To travel - Puteshestvovst' Путешествовать
Since - S С
First - Pervyy Первый
Time - Vremya Время
Times – Vremena Времена
Children - Deti Дети
Children - Rebyata ребята
Yours - Tvoyo Твоё

I need to drive the car very fast or very slowly
Mne nuzhno vodit' mashinu ochen' bystro ili ochen' medlenno
Мне нужно водить машину очень быстро или очень медленно
It is cold in the library
Kholodno v biblioteke
Холодно в библиотеке
I like to eat a hot meal for my lunch.
YA lyublyu yest' goryachuyu yedu na obed.
Я люблю есть горячую еду на обед.
I want to travel the world.
YA khochu puteshestvovat' po miru.
Я хочу путешествовать по миру.
Since the first time
Poskol'ku v pyervyy raz
Поскольку в первый раз
The children are yours
Deti tvoi
Дети твои

To answer - Otvetit' Ответить
To fly - Letat' Летать
To learn - Uchit'sya Учиться
To swim - Plavat' Плавать
To practice - Praktika Практика
To play - Igrat' Играть
To leave - Vyyti Выйти
Many/much/a lot - Mnogiye Многие
I go to - Ya idu v Я иду в
To leave (something) - Ostavlyat Оставлять
Against - Protiv Против

I am against him
Ya protiv nego
Я против него
I need to answer many questions
Mne nuzhno otvetit' na mnogiye voprosy
Мне нужно ответить на многие вопросы
I want to fly today
Ya khochu letet' segodnya
Я хочу лететь сегодня
I need to learn to swim
Mne nuzhno nauchit'sya plavat'
Мне нужно научиться плавать
I want to learn how to play better tennis.
YA khochu nauchit'sya igrat' luchshe v tennis.
Я хочу научиться играть лучше в теннис.
Everything is about the money.
Vse delo v den'gakh.
Все дело в деньгах.
I want to leave my dog at home.
YA khochu ostavit' svoyu sobaku doma.
Я хочу оставить свою собаку дома.

Nobody - Nikto Никто
Us - Nam Нам
We - My мы
To visit – Vizit Визит
To give - Dat' Дать
Which – Kakoy Какой
To meet – Vstrechat Встречать
Someone - Kto-to Кто-то
Just - Tol'ko Только
To walk - Khodit' Ходить
Family - Sem'ya Семья
Than - Chem Чем
Nothing - Nichego Ничего
Week - Nedelya Неделя

Something is better than nothing
Chto-to luchshe chem nichego
Что-то лучше чем ничего
We go each week to visit my family
My idem kazhduyu nedelyu navestit' moyu sem'yu
Мы идем каждую неделю навестить мою семью
I need to give you something
Mne nuzhno dat' tebe chto-to
Мне нужно дать тебе что-то
Do you want to meet someone?
Vy khotite videt' kago-to?
Вы хотите видеть кого-то?

*In Russian, tebe тебе / vam вам is the indirect object pronoun of the pronoun "you," the person who is actually affected by the action that is being carried out. However, tebe тебе is the informal form and vam вам is the formal form.

Friend – Drug Друг
To borrow - Vzat' Взять
To borrow - Odolzhit' одолжить
To look like - Vyglyadet' kak Выглядеть как
Grandfather - Dedushka Дедушка
To want - Khotet' Хотеть
To stay - Ostat'sya Остаться
To continue - Prodolzhat' Продолжать
Way - Put' (road)Путь
Way - Kuda (method) куда
That's why - Vot pochemu Вот почему
I am not going - Ya ne idu Я не иду

Do you want to look like Arnold
Ty khochesh vyglyadet' kak Arnol'd
Ты хочешь выглядеть как Арнольд
I want to borrow this book for my grandfather
Ya khochu vzyat' etu knigu dlya moyego dedushki
Я хочу взять эту книгу для моего дедушки
I want to drive and to continue on this way to my house
Ya khochu dvigat'sya i prodolzhat' idti po etomu puti do moyego doma
Я хочу двигаться и продолжать идти по этому пути до моего дома
I want to stay in St. Petersburg because I have a friend there.
YA khochu ostat'sya v Sankt-Peterburge, potomu chto u menya tam yest' drug.
Я хочу остаться в Санкт-Петербурге, потому что у меня там есть друг.

*Etomu Этому is the dative case of the demonstrative pronoun "this."

*"I want" / ya khochu я хочу and "you want" ty khochesh' ты хочешь.

The Program

I have - U menya yest' У меня есть
I have - Ya imeyu я имею
Don't – Ne Не
To show - Pokazat' Показать
To prepare - Podgotovit' Подготовить
How – Kak Как
Also / too / as well - Takzhe Также
Around – Vokrug Вокруг
Russian – Russkiy Русский

I don't want to see anyone here
Ya ne khochu nikogo videt' zdes'
Я не хочу никого видеть здесь
I need to show you how to prepare breakfast
Mne nuzhno pokazat' vam, kak prigotovit' zavtrak
Мне нужно показать вам, как приготовить завтрак
Why don't you have the book?
Pochemu u tebya net knigi?
Почему у тебя нет книги?
I don't need the car today
Mne ne nuzhna mashina segodnya
Мне не нужна машина сегодня
I am here also on Wednesdays
Ya zdes' takzhe po sredam
Я здесь также по средам
You do this every day?
Ty delayesh eto kazhdyy den'?
Ты делаешь это каждый день?
You need to walk around the school.
Vam nuzhno proytis' po shkole.
Вам нужно пройтись по школе.

*In Russian, moyego моего is the masculine and plural accusative form as well as the genitive masculine and neutral form of the pronoun "my."

Hour - Chas Час
Dark - Temno Темно
Darkness - temnota темнота
About - O О
Grandmother - Babushka Бабушка
Five - Pyat' Пять
Minute - Minuta Минута
Minutes - Minuty минуты
More - Bol'she Больше
To think - Dumat' Думать
To come - Priyekhat' Приехать
To hear - Uslyshat' Услышать
Last – Posledniy Последний
To talk / to speak - Govorit' Говорить

This is the last hour of darkness
Eto posledniy chas t'my
Это последний час тьмы
I want to come with you.
YA khochu poyti s toboy.
Я хочу пойти с тобой.
I can hear my grandmother speaking Russian.
YA slyshu, kak moya babushka govorit po-russki.
Я слышу, как моя бабушка говорит по-русски.
I need to think about this more.
Mne nuzhno podumat' ob etom bol'she.
Мне нужно подумать об этом больше.
From here to there, it's only five minutes
Otsyuda do tuda pyat' minut
Отсюда до туда пять минут

*In Russian, "from here" is otsyuda отсюда.

*Etom Этом is the prepositional case of the demonstrative pronoun "this."

The Program

To leave - Uyti Уйти
To bring - Prinesti Принести
To try - Popytat'sya Попытаться
To rent - Arendovat' Арендовать
Without her - Bez neyo Без неё
We are - My Мы
To turn off - Vyklyuchit' Выключить
To ask - Sprosit' Спросить
To stop - Ostanovit' Остановить
Permission - Razresheniye Разрешение

He must go and rent a house at the beach.
On dolzhen poyti i snyat' dom na beregu.
Он должен пойти и снять дом на берегу.
I need to turn off the lights early tonight
Vecherom ya dolzhen vyklyuchit' svet rano
Вечером я должен выключить свет рано
We want to stop here
My khotim ostanovitsya zdes'
Мы хотим остановиться здесь
We are from Moscow.
My iz Moskvy.
Мы из Москвы.
Your doctor is in the same building.
Vash vrach nakhoditsya v tom zhe zdanii.
Ваш врач находится в том же здании.
In order to leave you have to ask permission.
Chtoby uyti, nuzhno sprosit' razresheniya.
Чтобы уйти, нужно спросить разрешения.
Come here quickly.
Idi syuda bystro.
Иди сюда быстро.

*In Russian, the definition of na на is "at the."

To return - Vernut'sya Вернуться
Future - Budushcheye Будущее
Door - Dver' Дверь
Our - Nash Наш
On - Na На
Name - Imya Имя
Last name - Familiya Фамилия
Nice to meet you - Priyatno poznakomit'sya Приятно познакомиться

Nice to meet you, what is your name and your last name?
Priyatno poznakomit'sya s vami, kak vashe imya i vasha familiya?
Приятно познакомиться с вами, как ваше имя и ваша фамилия?
We can hope for a better future.
My mozhem nadeyat'sya na luchsheye budushcheye.
Мы можем надеяться на лучшее будущее.
It is impossible to live without problems.
Nevozmozhno zhit' bez problem.
Невозможно жить без проблем.
I want to return to the United States.
YA khochu vernut'sya v Soyedinennyye Shtaty.
Я хочу вернуться в Соединенные Штаты.
Why are you sad right now?
Pochemu ti grustnaya seychas?
Почему ты грустная сейчас?
Our house is on the mountain.
Nash dom nakhoditsya na gore.
Наш дом находится на горе.

*In Russian, po по means "on."

*This isn't a phrase book! The purpose of this book is solely to provide you with the tools to create your own sentences!

The Program

To happen - Sluchit'sya Случиться
To order - Zakazat' Заказать
Excuse me - Izvinite Извините
Child - Rebyonok Ребёнок
Woman - Zhenshchina Женщина
To begin / To start - Nachat' Начать
To finish - Zakonchit' Закончить
To remember - Zapomnit' Запомнить
Number – Nomer Номер

I need to remember this number
Mne nuzhno pomnit' etot nomer
Мне нужно помнить этот номер
This must happen today
Eto dolzhno proizoyti segodnya
Это должно произойти сегодня
Excuse me, my child is here as well
Izvinite, moy rebyonok tozhe zdes'
Извините, мой ребёнок тоже здесь
I want to order a soup.
YA khochu zakazat' sup.
Я хочу заказать суп.
We want to start the class soon.
My khotim poskoreye nachat' zanyatiya.
Мы хотим поскорее начать занятия.
In order to finish at three o'clock this afternoon, I need to finish soon.
Chtoby zakonchit' v tri chasa dnya, mne nuzhno zakonchit' kak mozhno skoreye.
Чтобы закончить в три часа дня, мне нужно закончить как можно скорее.
I want to learn how to speak Russian perfectly.
YA khochu nauchit'sya govorit' po-russki v sovershenstve.
Я хочу научиться говорить по-русски в совершенстве.

To smoke - Kurit' Курить
To love - Lubit' Любить
To help - Pomoch' Помочь
Sun - Solntse Солнце
Exact - Tochnyy Точный
Again - Opyat' Опять
Again - snova снова
I don't - Ya ne Я не

I don't want to smoke again
Ya ne khochu kurit' opyat'
Я не хочу курить опять
I want to help
Ya khochu pomoch'
Я хочу помочь
I love you
Ya tebya lyublyu
Я тебя люблю
I see you
Ya tebya vizhu
Я тебя вижу
I need you
Ty mne nuzhen
Ты мне нужен
There is sun outside today.
Segodnya na ulitse solntse.
Сегодня на улице солнце.
Is it possible to know the exact day?
Mozhno uznat' tochnyy den'?
Можно узнать точный день?

*In Russian, tebya тебя is the "direct object pronoun" of the pronoun you.

The Program

To read - Chitat' Читать
To write - Pisat' Писать
To teach - Uchit' Учить
To close - Zakryt' Закрыть
To turn on - Vklyuchit' Включить
To prefer - Predpochitat' Предпочитать
To put - Polozhit' Положить
Less - Men'she Меньше
Month - Mesyats Месяц
I talk - Ya govoryu Я говорю
To choose - Vybirat' Выбирать
In order to - Chtoby Чтобы

I need this book to learn how to read and write in Russian.
Mne nuzhna eta kniga, chtoby nauchit'sya chitat' i pisat' po-russki.
Мне нужна эта книга, чтобы научиться читать и писать по-русски.
I want to teach English in Russian.
YA khochu prepodavat' angliyskiy na russkom yazyke.
Я хочу преподавать английский на русском языке.
I want turn on the lights and close the door.
YA khochu vklyuchit' svet i zakryt' dver'.
Я хочу включить свет и закрыть дверь.
I want to pay less than you.
YA khochu platit' men'she, chem vy.
Я хочу платить меньше, чем вы.
I prefer to put this here.
YA predpochitayu razmeshchat' eto zdes'.
Я предпочитаю размещать это здесь.
I speak with the boy and the girl in Russian
Ya govoryu s mal'chikom i devochkoy po-russki
Я говорю с мальчиком и девочкой по-русски

To exchange - Pomenyat' Поменять
To call - Pozvonit' Позвонить
Brother - Brat Брат
Dad - Papa Папа
To sit - Sidet' Сидеть
Together - Vmeste Вместе
To change - Pomenyat' Поменять
Of course - Konechno Конечно
Welcome - Dobro pozhalovat' Добро пожаловать
During - Vo vremya Во время
Years - Gody Годы
Up - Naverkh Наверх
Down - Vniz Вниз
Big - Bol'shoy Большой
New - Novyy Новый
Never - Nikogda Никогда

I am never able to exchange this money at the bank.
YA nikogda ne smogu obmenyat' eti den'gi v banke.
Я никогда не смогу обменять эти деньги в банке.
I want to call my brother and my dad today
Segodnya ya khochu pozvonit' moemu bratu i moemy pape
Сегодня я хочу позвонить моему брату и моему папе
Of course I can come to the theater, and I want to sit together with you and with your sister
Konechno, ya mogu priyti v teatr, i ya khochu sidet' vmeste s toboy i s tvoyey sestroy
Конечно, я могу прийти в театр, и хочу сидеть вместе с тобой и с твоей сестрой
If you look under the table, you can see the new rug.
Yesli zaglyanut' pod stol, to mozhno uvidet' novyy kover.
Если заглянуть под стол, то можно увидеть новый ковер.

The Program

To allow - Razreshit' Разрешить
To believe - Verit' Верить
Morning – Utro Утро
Except - Krome Кроме
To promise - Obeshchat' Обещать
Good night - Spokoynoy nochi Спокойной ночи
To recognize - Priznat' Признать
People - Lyudi Люди
Far - Daleko Далеко
To move (to a place) - Pereyekhat' Переехать`
Sorry - Izvini Извини
To follow - Sledovat' Следовать
Sky - Nebo Небо
To go - Yekhat' Ехать

I need to allow him to go with us.
YA dolzhen pozvolit' yemu poyti s nami.
Я должен позволить ему пойти с нами.
I can't recognize him.
YA ne mogu uznat' yego.
Я не могу узнать его.
I believe everything except for this
Ya veryu vsemu krome etogo
Я верю всему кроме этого
I am sorry.
Mne zhal'.
Мне жаль.
I can see the sky from the window
Ya vizhu nebo iz okna
Я вижу небо из окна
The dog wants to follow me to the store.
Sobaka khochet poyti za mnoy v magazin.
Собака хочет пойти за мной в магазин.

Man - Muschina Мащина
To enter - Voyti Войти
To receive - Poluchit' Получить
Tonight - Vecherom Вечером
Through - Cherez Через
Him / his – Yego Его
To move - Dvigat'sya Двигаться
Different - Drugoy Другой
To open - Otkryt' Открыть
To buy - Kupit' Купить

I need to open the door for my sister
Mne nujno otkryt' dver' dlya moyey sestry
Мне нужно открыть дверь для моей сестры
I need to buy something
Mne nuzhno chto-to kupit'
Мне нужно что-то купить
He is a different man now.
On teper' drugoy chelovek.
Он теперь другой человек.
I need to move your cat to another chair
Ya dolzhen posadit' vashu koshku na drugoy stul
Я должен посадить вашу кошку на другой стул
I see the sun in the morning from the kitchen
Ya vizhu solntse po utram na kukhne
Я вижу солнце по утрам на кухне
I go into the house from the front entrance and not through the yard.
YA zakhozhu v dom s paradnogo vkhoda, a ne cherez dvor.
Я захожу в дом с парадного входа, а не через двор.

The Program

To pay - Platit' Платить
Without - Bez Без
Sister - Sestra Сестра
To hope - Nadeyat'sya Надеяться
To live - Zhit' Жить
Mom – Mama Мама
Mother - Mat' мать
To wish - Zhelat' Желать
Bad - Plokhoy Плохой
To get - Poluchit' Получить
To forget - Zabyt' Забыть
Everybody / Everyone - Vse Все
Although - Khotya Хотя
To feel - Chuvstvovat' Чувствовать
Great - Bol'shoy Большой
To like - Nravitsya Нравиться
In front - Speredi Спереди

I want to meet your brothers.
YA khochu poznakomit'sya s tvoimi brat'yami.
Я хочу познакомиться с твоими братьями.
I don't want to wish anything bad
Ya ne khochu zhelat' nichego plokhogo
Я не хочу желать ничего плохого
I must forget everybody from my past.
YA dolzhen zabyt' vsekh iz moyego proshlogo.
Я должен забыть всех из моего прошлого.
To feel well I must take vitamins.
Chtoby chuvstvovat' sebya khorosho, ya dolzhen prinimat' vitaminy.
Чтобы чувствовать себя хорошо, я должен принимать витамины.

*In Russian, nravitsya нравится means "to enjoy," while lyublyu люблю means "to love."

Person - Chelovek Человек
Behind - Za За
Well – Khorosho Хорошо
Restaurant - Restoran Ресторан
Bathroom - Vannaya komnata Ванная комната
Bathroom - Tualet туалет
Goodbye Do svidaniya До свидания
Next - Sleduyushchiy Следующий

Goodbye my friend.
Proshchay moy drug.
Прощай мой друг.
Which is the best restaurant in the area?
Kakoy luchshiy restoran v etom rayone?
Какой лучший ресторан в этом районе?
I can feel the heat.
YA chuvstvuyu zhar.
Я чувствую жар.
I need to repair a part of the cabinet in the bathroom.
Mne nuzhno otremontirovat' chast' shkafa v vannoy.
Мне нужно отремонтировать часть шкафа в ванной.
I want a car before the next year
Ya khochu mashinu na sleduyushchiy god
Я хочу машину на следующий год
I like the house, however it is very small
 Mne nravitsa dom, no on ochen' malen'kiy
Мне нравится дом, но он очень маленький
I am close to the person behind you
Ya blizhe k cheloveku za toboy
Я ближе к человеку за тобой

*In Russian, sleduyushchiy следующий means "next to," for example, "I am next to him". While sleduyushcheye следующее means "the following," for example "the next exit."

The Program

Please - Pozhaluysta Пожалуйста
To remove - Udalyat' Удалять
Beautiful - Krasivyy Красивый
To lift - Podnyat' Поднять
Include - Vklucheno, Включено
Including - Vkluchaya включая
Belong - Otsyuda Отсюда
To hold - Derzhat' Держать
To check - Proveryat' Проверять
Small - Malen'kaya Маленькая / **Small** - Malen'kiy маленький

She wants to remove this door
Ona khochet snyat' etu dver'
Она хочет снять эту дверь
We need to check the size of the house
Mne nuzhno proverit' razmery doma
Мне нужно проверить размеры дома
I want to lift this.
YA khochu podnyat' eto.
Я хочу поднять это.
Can you please put the wood in the fire?
Ne mogli by vy podlozhit' drova v ogon'?
Не могли бы вы подложить дрова в огонь?
This doesn't belong here, I need to check again
Eto ne otsyuda, mne nuzhno proverit' opyat'
Это не отсюда, мне нужно проверить опять

*In Russian the verb "need" has two definitions nado надо and nuzhno нужно. Both signify doing something out of necessity such as "need to," "have to," "should." Both could be used interchangeably however nado надо has more of a colloquial use. On the other hand, dolzhen должен means "must", something you are forced to do. You will notice in some instances, throughout the program, these three Russian verbs being used interchangeably.

Real - Nastoyashchiy Настоящий
Week - Nedelya Неделя
Size - Razmer Размер
Even though - Dazhe yesli Даже если
Doesn't - Net Нет
So - Tak Так
So - Normal'no нормально
Price – Tsena Цена

Is that a real diamond?
Eto nastoyashchiy brilliant?
Это настоящий бриллиант?
This week the weather was very beautiful
Na etoy nedele pogoda byla ochen' khoroshaya
На этой неделе погода была очень хорошая
The sun is high in the sky.
Solntse vysoko v nebe.
Солнце высоко в небе.
I can pay this although the price is expensive
Ya mogu zaplatit' za eto, khotya tsena dorogaya
Я могу заплатить за это, хотя цена дорогая
Can you please hold my hand?
Ne mogli by vy derzhat' menya za ruku?
Не могли бы вы держать меня за руку?
Is everything included in this price?
V etu tsenu vsyo vklucheno?
В эту цену всё включено?

*In Russian, both tak так and normal'no нормально are used to indicate "so". However tak так definition of "so" is used to express cases such as "so much", or "so big." While normal'no нормально definition of "so" is used to indicate "then."

Building Bridges

In Building Bridges, we take the six conjugated verbs that have been selected after studies I have conducted for several months in order to determine which verbs are most commonly conjugated, and which are then automatically followed by an infinitive verb. For example, once you know how to say, "I need," "I want," "I can," and "I like," you will be able to connect words and say almost anything you want more correctly and understandably.

I want - Ya khochu Я хочу
I need - Mne nuzhno / mne nado Мне нужно / мне надо
I can - Ya mogu Я могу
I like - Mne nravitsya Мне нравится
I go - Ya idu Я иду
I have to/ I must - Ya dolzhen Я должен
To have - U menya yest' У меня есть

I want to go to my apartment
Ya khochu poyti v moyu kvartiru
Я хочу пойти в мою квартиру
I can go with you to the bus station
Ya mogu poyti s toboy na avtobusnuyu stantsiyu
Я могу пойти с тобой на автобусную станцию
I need to walk outside the museum.
Mne nuzhno vyyti za predely muzeya.
Мне нужно выйти за пределы музея.
I like to eat oranges.
YA lyublyu yest' apel'siny.
Я люблю есть апельсины.
I want to teach a class
Ya khochu uchit' klass
Я хочу учить класс
I have to speak to my teacher
Ya dolzhen pogovorit' s moim uchitelem
Я должен поговорить с моим учителем

Please master *every* single page up until here prior to attempting the following two pages!

You want - Ty khochesh' Ты хочешь
Do you want? - Khochesh' li ty? хочешь ли ты?
He wants - On khochet Он хочет
Does he want? - Khochet li on? хочет ли он?
She wants - Ona khochet Она хочет
Does she want? - Khochet li ona? хочет ли она?
We want - My khotim Мы хотим
Do we want? - Khotim li my? хотим ли мы?
They want - Oni khotyat Они хотят
Do they want? - Khotyat li oni? хотят ли они?
You (plural/ formal sing) want - Vy khotite Вы хотите

You need - Tebe nuzhno Тебе нужно
Do you need? - Nuzhno li tebe? Нужно ли тебе?
He needs - Yemu nuzhno Ему нужно
Does he need? - Nuzhno li yemu? Нужно ли ему?
She needs - Yey nuzhno Ей нужно
Does she need? - Nuzhno li yey? Нужно ли ей?
We need - Nam nuzhno Нам нужно
Do we need? - Nuzhno li nam? Нужно ли нам?
They need - Im nuzhno Им нужно
Do they need? Nuzhno li im? Нужно ли им?
You (plural/ formal sing) need - Vam nuzhno Вам нужно

You can - Ty mozhesh Ты можешь
Can you? - Mozhesh li ty? Можешь ли ты?
He can - On mozhet Он может
Can he? - Mozhet li on? Может ли он?
She can - Ona mozhet Она может
Can she? - Mozhet li ona? Может ли она?
We can - My mozhem Мы можем
Can we? - Mozhem li my? Можем ли мы?

The Program

They can - Oni mogut Они могут
Can they? - Mogut li oni? Могут ли они?
You (plural/ formal sing) can - Vy mozhete Вы можете

You like - Tebe nravitsya Тебе нравится
do you like? - Nravitsya li tebe? Нравится ли тебе?
He likes - Yemu nravitsya Ему нравится
does he like? - Nravitsya li yemu? Нравится ли ему?
She like - Yey nravitsya Ей нравится
does she like? - Nravitsya li yey? Нравится ли ей?
We like - Nam nravitsya Нам нравится
do we like? - Nravitsya li nam? Нравится ли нам?
They like - Im nravitsya Им нравится
do they like? - Nravitsya li im? Нравится ли им?
You (plural/ formal sing) like - Vam nravitsya Вам нравится

You go - Ty idyosh' Ты идёшь
Do you go? - Idyosh' li ty? Идёшь ли ты?
He goes - On idyot Он идёт
Does he go? - Idyot li on? Идёт ли он?
She goes - Ona idyot Она идёт
Does she go? - Idyot li ona? Идёт ли она?
We go - My idyom Мы идём
Do we go? - Idyom li my? Идём ли мы?
They go - Oni idut Они идут
Do they go? - Idut li oni? Идут ли они?
You (plural/ formal sing) go - Vy idyote Вы идёте

You must - Ty dolzhen Ты должен
Do you have to - Dolzhen li ty? Должен ли ты?
He must - On dolzhen Он должен
Does he have to - Dolzhen li on? Должен ли он?
She must - Ona dolzhna Она должна
Does she have to - Dolzhna li ona? Должна ли она?
We have - My dolzhni Мы должны
Do we have to - Dolzhni li my? Должны ли мы?
They must - Oni dolzhni Они должны
Do they have to - Dolzhni li oni? Должны ли они?
You (plural/ formal sing) must - Vy dolzhni Вы должны

You have - Ty imeyesh Ты имеешь
You have - U tebya yest' у тебя есть
He has - On i'meyet Он имеет
He has - U nego yest' у него есть
She has - Ona i'meyet Она имеет
She has - U neyo yest' у неё есть
We have - My imeyem Мы имеем
We have - U nas yest' у нас есть
They have - Oni imeyut Они имеют
They have - U nikh yest' у них есть
You (plural) have - Vy imeyete Вы имеете
You (plural) have - U vas yest' у вас есть

The Program

Do you want to go?
Khotite li vy poyti?
Хотите ли вы пойти?

Does he want to fly?
Khochet li on letet'?
Хочет ли он лететь?

We want to swim
My khotim plavat'
Мы хотим плавать

Do they want to run?
Khotyat li oni begat'?
Хотят ли они бегать?

Do you need to clean?
Dolzhna li ty ubrat'?
Должна ли ты убрать?

She needs to sing a song
Ona doljna pet' pesnyu
Она должна петь песню

We need to travel
My dolzhny puteshestvovat'
Мы должны путешествовать

They don't need to fight
Oni ne dolzhny drat'sya
Они не должні драться

You (plural) need to save your money.
Vam nuzhno ekonomit' den'gi.
Вам нужно экономить деньги.

Can you hear me?
Slyshish li ty menya?
Слышишь ли ты меня?

He can dance very well
On mozhet tantsevat' ochen' khorosho
Он может танцевать очень хорошо

We can go out tonight
Me mozhem poyti segodnya vecherom
Мы можем пойти сегодня вечером

The fireman can break the door during an emergency.
Pozharnyy mozhet slomat' dver' vo vremya chrezvychaynoy situatsii.
Пожарный может сломать дверь во время чрезвычайной ситуации.

Do you like to eat here?
Nravitsya li vam zdes' est'?
Нравится ли вас здесь есть?

He likes to spend time here
On lyubit provodit' vremya zdes'
Он любит проводить время здесь

We like to fix the house
My khoteli ispravit' dom
Мы хотели исправть дом

They like to cook
Oni lyubyat gotovit'
Они любят готовить

You (plural) like to play soccer.
Vy lyubite igrat' v futbol.
Вы любите играть в футбол.

The Program

Do you go to the movies on weekends?
Khodite li vy v kino po vykhodnym?
Ходите ли вы в кино по выходным?

He goes fishing
On idyot lovit' rybu
Он идёт ловить рыбу

We are going to relax
My sobirayemsya rasslabit'sya
Мы собираемся расслабиться

They go out to eat at a restaurant every day.
Oni khodyat poyest' v restoran kazhdyy den'.
Они ходят поесть в ресторан каждый день.

Do you have money?
Yest' li u tebya den'gi?
Есть ли у тебя деньги?

She must look outside
Ona dolzhna posmoret' snaruzhi
Она должна посмотреть снаружи

We have to sign here
My dolzhny raspisat'sya zdes'
Мы должны расписаться здесь

They have to send the letter
Oni dolzhny otpravit' pis'mo
Они должны отправить письмо

You (plural) have to stand in line.
Vy dolzhny stoyat' v ocheredi.
Вы должны стоять в очереди.

Other Useful Tools in the Russian Language

Days of the Week
Sunday - Voskresen'ye Воскресенье
Monday - Ponedel'nik Понедельник
Tuesday – Vtornik Вторник
Wednesday – Sreda Среда
Thursday – Chetverg Четверг
Friday – Pyatnitsa Пятница
Saturday – Subbota Суббота
Seasons
Spring - Vesna Весна
Summer – Leto Лето
Autumn – Osen' Осень
Winter – Zima Зима

Colors
Black – Chyornyy Чёрный
White - Belyy Белый
Gray - Seryy Серый
Red - Krasnyy Красный
Blue - Siniy Синий
Yellow – Zhyoltyy Жёлтый
Green - Zelyonyy Зелёный
Orange - Orazhevyy Оранжевый
Purple - Fioletovyy Фиолетовый
Brown – Korichnevyy Коричневый

Cardinal Directions
North - Sever Север
South - Yug Юг
East - Vostok Восток
West - Zapad Запад

The Program

Numbers
One - Odin Один
Two - Dva Два
Three - Tri Три
Four - Chetyre Четыре
Five - Pyat' Пять
Six - Shest' Шесть
Seven - Sem' Семь
Eight - Vosem' Восемь
Nine - Devyat' Девять
Ten - Desyat' Десять

Transportation
Train - Poyest Поезд
Tram - Tramvay Трамвай
Airplane - Samalyot Самолёт
Car - Masheena Машина
Subway - Mytro Метро
Tram - Tramcai Трамвай
Bus - Aftoboos Автобус
Bus station - Автобусная остановка Avtobusnaya ostanovka
Trolleybus - Tralleybus Троллейбус
Cab/taxi - Taksee Такси
Bicycle - Velosiped Велосипед
Scooter - Samokat Самокат

Travel
Suitcase - Chee-ma-dan Чемодан
Luggage - Ba-gash Багаж
Reservation - Ree-zeer-va-tsi-ya Резервация
Visa - Vee-za Виза
Passport - Pas-part Паспорт
Customs - Ta-mozh-nya Таможня
Tourist - Too-reest Турист (masculine)
Tourist - Too-reest-ka Туристка (feminine)

Congratulations Now You're on Your Own

If you merely absorb the required three hundred and fifty words in this book, you will then have acquired the basis to become conversational in Russian! After memorizing these three hundred and fifty words, this conversational foundational basis that you have just gained will trigger your ability to make improvements in conversational fluency at an amazing speed! However, in order to engage in quick and easy conversational communication, you need a special type of basics, and this book will provide you with just that.

Unlike the foreign language learning systems presently used in schools and universities, along with books and programs that are available on the market today, that focus on *everything* but being conversational, *this* method's sole focus is on becoming conversational in Russian as well as any other language. Once you have successfully mastered the required words in this book, there are two techniques that if combined with these essential words, can further enhance your skills and will result in you improving your proficiency tenfold. *However*, these two techniques will only succeed *if* you have completely and successfully absorbed the three hundred and fifty words. *After* you establish the basis for fluent communications by memorizing these words, you can enhance your conversational abilities even more if you use the following two techniques.

The first step is to attend a Russian language class that will enable you to sharpen your grammar. You will gain additional vocabulary and learn past and present tenses, and if you apply these skills that you learn in the class, together with the three hundred and fifty words that you have previously memorized, you will be improving your conversational skills tenfold. You will notice that, conversationally, you will succeed at a much higher rate than any of your classmates. A simple second technique is to choose Russian subtitles while watching a movie. If you have successfully mastered and grasped these three hundred and fifty words, then the combination of the two—those words along with the subtitles—will aid you considerably in putting all the grammar into perspective, and again, conversationally, you will improve tenfold.

Once you have established a basis of quick and easy conversation in Russian with those words that you just attained, every additional word or grammar rule you pick up from there on will be gravy. And these additional words or grammar rules can be combined with the three hundred and fifty words, enriching your conversational abilities even more. Basically, after the research and studies I've conducted with my method over the years, I came to the conclusion that in order to become conversational, you first must learn the words and *then* learn the grammar.

The Russian language is compatible with the mirror translation technique. Likewise, with *this* language, you can use this mirror translation technique in order to become conversational, enabling you to communicate even more effortlessly. Mirror translation is the method of translating a phrase or sentence, word for word from English to Russian, by using these imperative words that you have acquired through this program (such as the sentences I used in this book). Latin languages, Middle Eastern languages, and Slavic languages, along with a few others, are also compatible with the mirror translation technique. Though you won't be speaking perfectly proper and precise Russian, you will still be fully understood and, conversation-wise, be able to get by just fine.

NOTE FROM THE AUTHOR

Thank you for your interest in my work. I encourage you to share your overall experience of this book by posting a review. Your review can make a difference! Please feel free to describe how you benefited from my method or provide creative feedback on how I can improve this program. I am constantly seeking ways to enhance the quality of this product, based on personal testimonials and suggestions from individuals like you.

Thanks and best of luck,

Yatir Nitzany

Also by Yatir Nitzany

Conversational Spanish Quick and Easy

Conversational French Quick and Easy

Conversational Italian Quick and Easy

Conversational Portuguese Quick and Easy

Conversational German Quick and Easy

Conversational Dutch Quick and Easy

Conversational Norwegian Quick and Easy

Conversational Danish Quick and Easy

Conversational Russian Quick and Easy

Conversational Ukrainian Quick and Easy

Conversational Bulgarian Quick and Easy

Conversational Polish Quick and Easy

Conversational Hebrew Quick and Easy

Conversational Yiddish Quick and Easy

Conversational Armenian Quick and Easy

Conversational Romanian Quick and Easy

Conversational Arabic Quick and Easy
....

Conversational Arabic Quick and Easy
Lebanese Dialect
....

Conversational Arabic Quick and Easy
Syrian Dialect
....

Conversational Arabic Quick and Easy
Jordanian Dialect
....

Conversational Arabic Quick and Easy
Egyptian Dialect
....

Conversational Arabic Quick and Easy
Moroccan Dialect
....

Conversational Arabic Quick and Easy
Tunisian Dialect
....

Conversational Arabic Quick and Easy
Saudi (Hejazi, Najdi & Gulf) Dialect
....

Conversational Arabic Quick and Easy
Iraqi Dialect
....

Conversational Arabic Quick and Easy
Emirati Dialect
....

Conversational Arabic Quick and Easy
Qatari Dialect
....

www.ingramcontent.com/pod-product-compliance
Lightning Source LLC
Chambersburg PA
CBHW052106110526
44591CB00013B/2371